dinosaurs

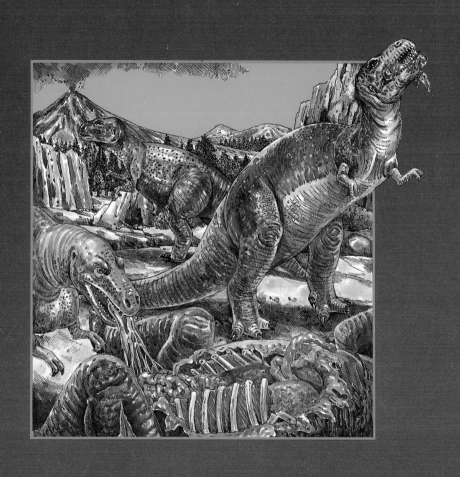

SERIES EDITOR   DAVID SALARIYA
BOOK EDITOR   APRIL McCROSKIE
CONSULTANT   JOHN COOPER

Published in 1995
by FranklinWatts
95 Madison Avenue
New York, NY 10016

© THE SALARIYA BOOK COMPANY LTD MCMXCV

Library of Congress Cataloging-in-Publication Data
Steedman, Scott.
  Dinosaurs / written by Scott Steedman ; illustrated by Carolyn Scrace.
    p. cm. – (Worldwise)
  Includes index.
  ISBN 0-531-14377-5 (lib. bdg.) ISBN 0-531-15283-9 (pbk.)
  1. Dinosaurs – Juvenile literature. [1. Dinosaurs.] I. Scrace, Carolyn, ill.
  II. Title. III. Series.
QE862.D5S635   1995   95-76
567.9'1 – dc20   CIP
Printed in Belgium   AC

worldwise
dinosaurs

Written by
SCOTT STEEDMAN
Illustrated by
CAROLYN SCRACE

Series Created & Designed by
DAVID SALARIYA

FRANKLIN WATTS
New York Chicago London Toronto Sydney

CONTENTS

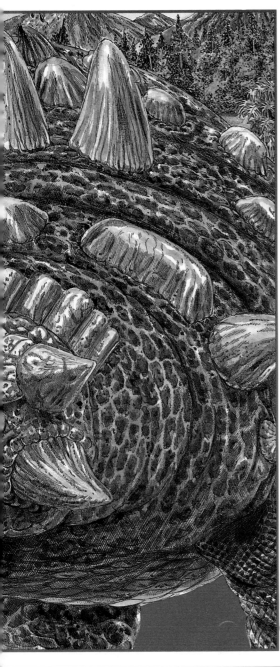

The Dinosaur Age

(the Mesozoic era) began 225 million years ago. At that time the earth was covered in thick forests, dusty plains, and shallow seas. The climate was much hotter than it is now. There were no mammals or birds. The first dinosaurs searched for food among the shrubs and trees. The dinosaurs were reptiles, and today's snakes and crocodiles with their scaly skin are close relatives. Dinosaurs survived on Earth for the next 160 million years.

People who study life-forms from the past are called paleontologists.

This worker is using a brush to clear away tiny fragments from a bone.

The bare bones are usually all that is left of a dinosaur. All the soft parts like the skin and organs have rotted away. Only the hardest bits of bones, teeth, and claws have turned to stone, or fossilized. Experts dig up these fragments in search of clues to help them put the beast together again. The size of one bone can tell us how big the dinosaur was. Ridges and grooves show how the muscles and blood vessels fitted together. One tooth may be enough to show what the animal ate. This giant jigsaw puzzle can take years to complete.

The first step in recreating the dinosaur is to dig up the bones. Workers chip away the rock that surrounds the skeleton.

Fossils are very fragile and must be treated with care. Bones are covered in tissue paper or wrapped in bandages.

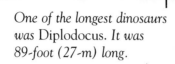

One of the longest dinosaurs was Diplodocus. *It was 89-foot (27-m) long.*

Dinosaurs are the largest animals to have walked on earth. The biggest ones weighed ten times more than the heaviest elephant. The smallest dinosaurs were no bigger than chickens. There were hundreds of different dinosaurs but not all of them lived at the same time.

The Mesozoic era was divided into 3 periods – Triassic, Jurassic, and Cretaceous.

Triassic period
245-208 million years ago

Jurassic period
208-146 million years ago

Cretaceous period
146-65 million years ago

The first dinosaurs appeared in the Triassic period, from 245 to 208 million years ago. The climate was dry and warm.

The biggest species appeared in the Jurassic period, from 208 to 146 million years ago. Earth was greener and more lush.

A huge variety of dinosaurs existed in the Cretaceous period, from 146 to 65 million years ago.

Pteranodon – *a flying reptile.*

Some experts believe birds – and not reptiles – are the dinosaurs' closest living relatives. The *Archaeopteryx* had reptile features, but it had feathers like a modern bird.

Modern pigeon

Some dinosaurs were meat eaters (carnivores), others were plant eaters (herbivores).

Deinonychus *was a fast-moving hunter.*

Stegosaurus

Modern crocodile

If we compare a modern crocodile to a Stegosaurus *we see some similarities. But the crocodile is smaller with legs that stick out sideways from its body.*

Carnivorous giants hunted

other dinosaurs – even if they were plant eaters much bigger than they were themselves. They would follow a herd of grazing herbivores, and then wait for a small or weak member of the pack to wander off on its own. The meat eaters then moved in for the kill.

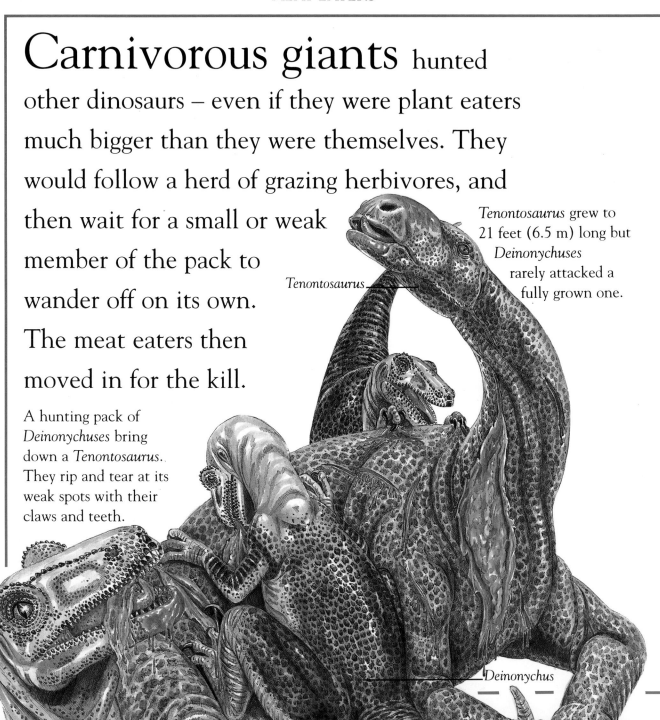

Tenontosaurus grew to 21 feet (6.5 m) long but *Deinonychuses* rarely attacked a fully grown one.

Tenontosaurus

A hunting pack of *Deinonychuses* bring down a *Tenontosaurus*. They rip and tear at its weak spots with their claws and teeth.

Deinonychus

The hunter had to move fast – the rotting flesh was very smelly and brought other dinosaurs running for their share.

Daspletosaurus was a smaller relative of *Tyrannosaurus*, reaching 30 feet (9 m) in length. It lived 75 to 65 million years ago in the Cretaceous period.

Albertosaurus

Albertosaurus also lived in the Cretaceous period and looked similar to *Daspletosaurus*. It hunted dinosaurs such as the *Triceratops*.

Daspletosaurus

Tyrannosaurus rex lived in the Cretaceous period, from 146 to 65 million years ago.

Tyrannosaurus rex

Tyrannosaurus rex probably hunted alone. But it may also have been a scavenger, joining other dinosaurs to finish off their kills.

Tyrannosaurus *attacks*

Triceratops *uses horns for defense.*

Struthiomimus *chases insects.*

Pachycephalosaurus *males butt heads.*

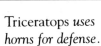

Resting on stomach

Starting to rise

Throwing head back

Fully upright

Massive jaws and teeth helped *Tyrannosaurus* to rip great chunks of flesh out of its prey. It did not chew its food, but swallowed it whole.

Tyrannosaurus sprinted after its prey on powerful back legs. The tail helped balance the weight of its massive head.

Tyrannosaurus rex was the biggest meat eater ever to walk on Earth. Its name means "king tyrant lizard." It grew 46 feet (14 m) long and 17 feet (5 m) tall. It hunted other dinosaurs, probably by hiding and then pouncing on them. It had a mouth full of nasty teeth and strong back legs with sharp claws.

Tyrannosaurus runs after a Parasaurolophus.

On pages 16 and 17, a *Compsognathus* chases its prey.

Resting on stomach *Starting to rise* *Throwing head back* *Fully upright*

Massive jaws and teeth helped *Tyrannosaurus* to rip great chunks of flesh out of its prey. It did not chew its food, but swallowed it whole.

Tyrannosaurus sprinted after its prey on powerful back legs. The tail helped balance the weight of its massive head.

Tyrannosaurus rex was the biggest meat eater ever to walk on Earth. Its name means "king tyrant lizard." It grew 46 feet (14 m) long and 17 feet (5 m) tall. It hunted other dinosaurs, probably by hiding and then pouncing on them. It had a mouth full of nasty teeth and strong back legs with sharp claws.

Tyrannosaurus *runs after a* Parasaurolophus.

On pages 16 and 17, a *Compsognathus* chases its prey.

15

The heavy tail could be lifted off the ground.

Plateosaurus *ate pebbles which helped grind up food in its stomach.*

Long neck

Living in a herd would have helped protect the *Plateosaurus* against attacks from predators.

The biggest dinosaurs were the vegetarians. A slow-moving creature like *Plateosaurus* had to eat a lot of plants every day just to survive. To digest all this, it needed an enormous stomach and intestines. But *Plateosaurus* was small compared to the real giants such as *Brachiosaurus*. This species weighed 80 tons and its neck was 30 feet (9 m) long.

Cheek pouch

Small head

A *Plateosaurus* could walk
on all four legs or by
standing up on its strong
back legs. Standing
upright it could stretch
its neck to feed on high
leaves that other
dinosaurs could not reach.

The thumb ended in a
broad, powerful claw.
Plateosaurus must
have used this
to fight off meat
eating dinosaurs.

Thumb
claw

Diamond-shaped plates

To protect its rear, Stegosaurus swished its tail spikes from side to side.

Strong pillar-like legs

Small, low-slung head

The plates were not used for defense. They had holes like a sponge and were probably rich in blood vessels. Some experts think that *Stegosaurus* used its plates like a radiator to heat up or cool down its body.

Stegosaurus means "plated lizard" because people used to think that the plates on its back overlapped like roof tiles.

A small brain meant that *Stegosaurus* moved slowly and that its senses and reflexes were poor. But this was not a great problem, and they were common for nearly 70 million years.

Tail spikes

Stegosaurus remains were found only in western North America, in what is now Colorado, Utah, and Wyoming. It lived about 150 million years ago in the late Jurassic period.

A *Stegosaurus* had a big body but a small brain. This lumbering dinosaur was 25 feet (7.5 m) long and weighed 1.5 tons, but its brain was the size of a walnut. A crest of jagged plates ran in a staggered line down its back. It also had long spikes on its tail, which it could swing around like a club.

Stegosaurus fed on ferns, cycads, and other low-level vegetation. It had small teeth and weak jaw muscles so it did not chew much. Instead, it had a huge stomach where food was left to ferment for several days.

Wide neck frill

Tongue

Powerful jaw

Five toes on front feet

Shorter front legs

Many dinosaurs laid eggs –
just like modern reptiles and birds.
This fact was proved in the 1920s, when
the nests of a colony of *Protoceratops* were
found in the Gobi Desert in Mongolia.
The female laid eggs in a hollow scooped out
in the sand. She then sat on them to keep them
warm. Turn the page to see a nest and hatchlings.

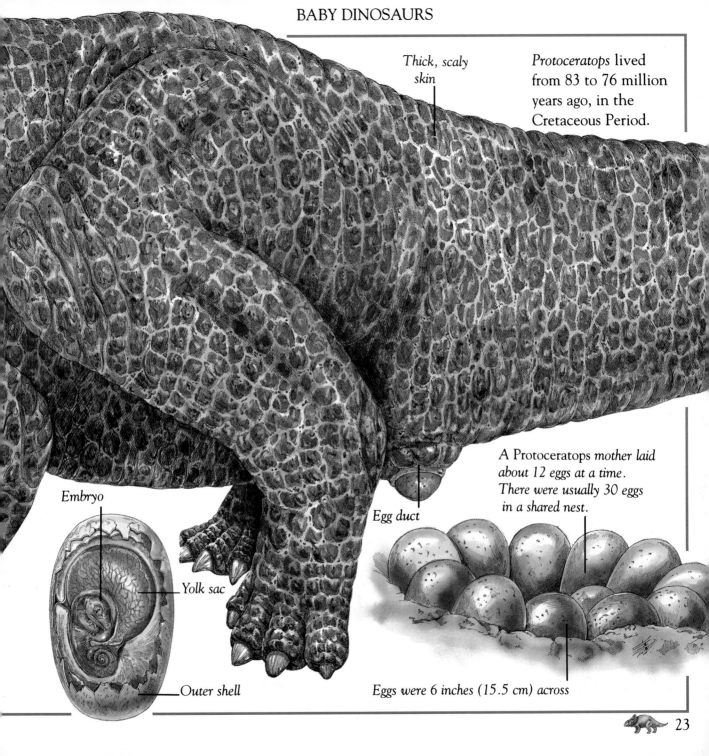

Thick, scaly skin

Protoceratops lived from 83 to 76 million years ago, in the Cretaceous Period.

Embryo

Yolk sac

Outer shell

Egg duct

A Protoceratops *mother laid about 12 eggs at a time. There were usually 30 eggs in a shared nest.*

Eggs were 6 inches (15.5 cm) across

23

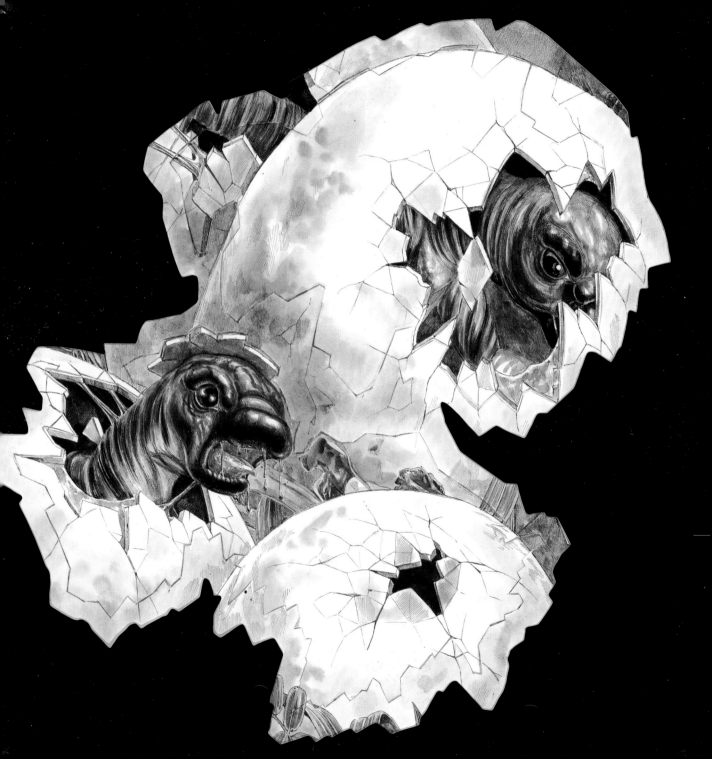

Maiasaura mothers had to be on the lookout for hungry dinosaurs who would eat their young. The mothers may even have shared babysitting duties.

Horny crest above the eyes

Maiasauras roamed the high plains of North America. Fossils suggest that tens of thousands of animals may have gathered together for safety in numbers.

Maiasaura *was a duck-billed dinosaur that could walk upright.*

It is likely that the fat end of the eggs, where the baby hatched, faced out of the nest. This way the baby *Maiasaura* could get out more easily.

Babies were born with small teeth and were able to eat solid food right away.

Like many modern mammals, baby Maiasauras *had large eyes.*

The *Maiasaura* nests were close together. The average distance between them was about 23 feet (7 m) – the length of a fully grown *Maiasaura* mother.

Fossilized nests and babies are very rare. This is probably because most dinosaurs built their nests in hard-to-reach places. The *Maiasaura* nests were discovered in 1978.

Mothers brought food for their young before they went out to forage for their own.

Finally the eggs hatched and

tiny, perfectly formed dinosaur babies came crawling out. The drawings on these pages show a nest of *Maiasaura* dinosaurs in Montana. This is how it may have looked 80 to 75 million years ago (Cretaceous period). Some of these babies would have been in the nest for weeks. Their parents brought them food, and sat on them to keep them warm.

Maiasaura means "good mother lizard." Dinosaur babies were not very big, but they grew quickly. When they left the nest, the babies may have walked in the center of the herd, so that they were protected by a ring of fully grown dinosaurs.

Deinonychus had a large head full of big jagged teeth. Its front legs ended in sharp, slender claws.

Horny beaks and sharp claws helped many dinosaurs to bite off vegetation or catch their prey. Plant eaters such as *Triceratops* and *Psittacosaurus* had toothless beaks to help them crunch through even the toughest tree trunks.

Deinonychus hunted slower-moving dinosaurs such as Hypsilophodon. *As its prey tired,* Deinonychus *leapt onto its back and ripped open its victim's soft belly.*

Psittacosaurus means "parrot lizard." This plant eater lived from 98 to 90 million years ago. It had a strong skull, a beak, and muscular jaws for chewing its food.

Psittacosaurus —

Oviraptor means "egg thief."

This small, fast-moving dinosaur had a horny beak and long, curving claws. They may have used these to crack open the eggs of other dinosaurs.

Oviraptor got its name because experts have always believed that this dinosaur ate the eggs of other dinosaurs.

There is no evidence that *Oviraptor* ate eggs of its own kind. Other dinosaurs such as *Coleophysis* ate their own babies.

Three-fingered hand

Broken dinosaur egg

Bony crest

Sharp prong

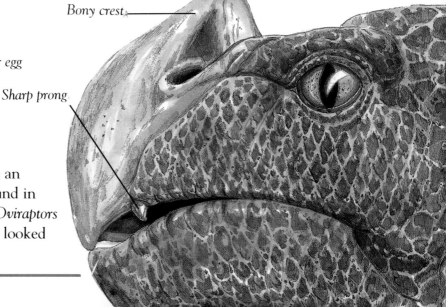

Experts recently discovered a fossilized *Oviraptor* egg. It was found near a place where an adult *Oviraptor* skeleton was found in 1923. Perhaps this means that *Oviraptors* were not egg thieves but simply looked after their own babies.

Euoplocephalus had a big, strong tail club that it used as a weapon in self-defense. If a meat-eating *Albertosaurus* kept attacking it, *Euoplocephalus* would swing its heavy tail at the attacker's legs. The *Albertosaurus* would be knocked to the ground. Crippled and helpless it would be eaten by other carnivorous dinosaurs.

The tail club was solid bone and was very heavy. The rest of the tail was relatively light, so the dinosaur could swing it freely.

Albertosaurus

Tail club

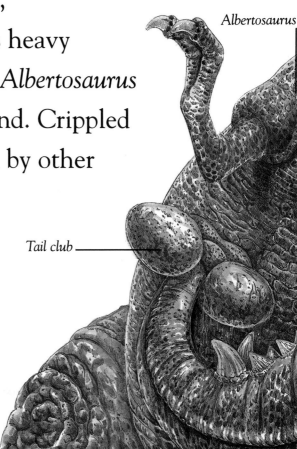

Kentrosaurus

Kentrosaurus was a small dinosaur covered with long spines. It would back into its attackers to defend itself.

One of the best ways to avoid being eaten was to run away! Lesothosaurus was small and moved very quickly.

To protect their babies, a herd of Chasmosauruses would form a circle. Predators would see just horns and armored plates.

Euoplocephalus

Euoplocephalus was armored heavily. Its head was covered with spikes and spines, and bony plates pricked out of its back and tail.

31

Triceratops lived in North America 70 million years ago. It lived at the same time as giant predators such as *Tyrannosaurus*. It grew to 30 feet (9 m) long and weighed 5.4 tons.

With its massive horns, Styracosaurus was one of the strangest looking dinosaurs.

Horns could reach 5 feet (1.5 m) long.

Open woodland

Thick, scaly skin

Single nose horn

Heavy tail

Stubby legs

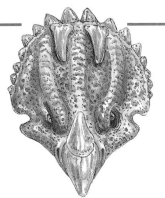

Centrosaurus

Centrosaurus was another ceratopsid dinosaur. This meant that it had a collection of horns and spikes.

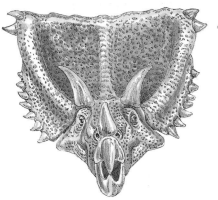

Chasmosaurus

The huge neck frill protected the animal's back as well as anchored its strong jaw muscles. This is *Chasmosaurus*.

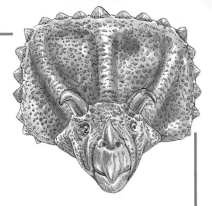

Anchiceratops

Anchiceratops had three large horns. It was a close relative of *Triceratops*. It moved slowly around the woodlands of western North America.

Triceratops had a huge head

armed with three sharp horns – one above each eye and a third on the tip of its nose. It also had a neck frill lined with bony spikes. These spikes were purely for protection. *Triceratops* and its many relatives were slow-moving vegetarians who did not attack other dinosaurs for food. They used their large horny beaks to snip off plant stems and shoots.

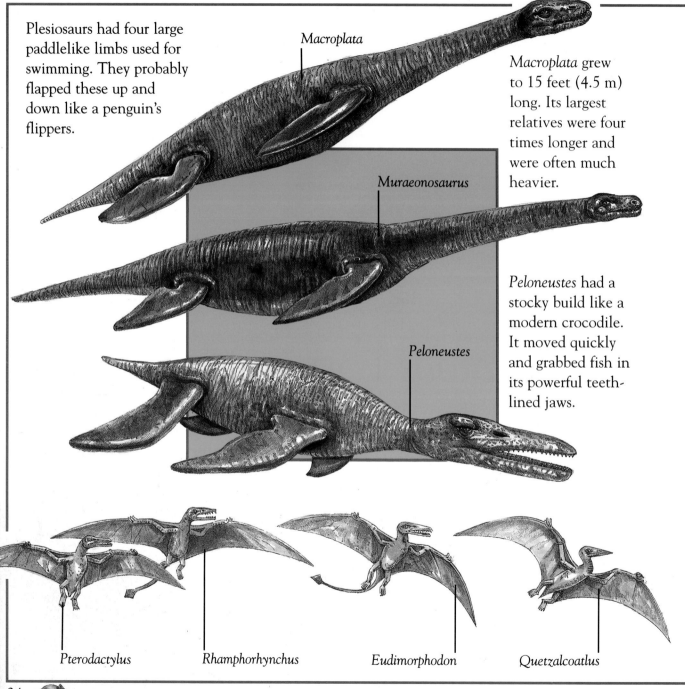

Plesiosaurs had four large paddlelike limbs used for swimming. They probably flapped these up and down like a penguin's flippers.

Macroplata

Macroplata grew to 15 feet (4.5 m) long. Its largest relatives were four times longer and were often much heavier.

Muraeonosaurus

Peloneustes had a stocky build like a modern crocodile. It moved quickly and grabbed fish in its powerful teeth-lined jaws.

Peloneustes

Pterodactylus

Rhamphorhynchus

Eudimorphodon

Quetzalcoatlus

In prehistoric times, flying

and swimming reptiles filled the seas and skies.
Though they were not dinosaurs, they were
related to these land-bound giants.
The pterosaurs were the only reptiles that
could fly. Sea reptiles included massive turtles,
ichthyosaurs (fish reptiles), and long-necked
monsters called plesiosaurs (ribbon reptiles).

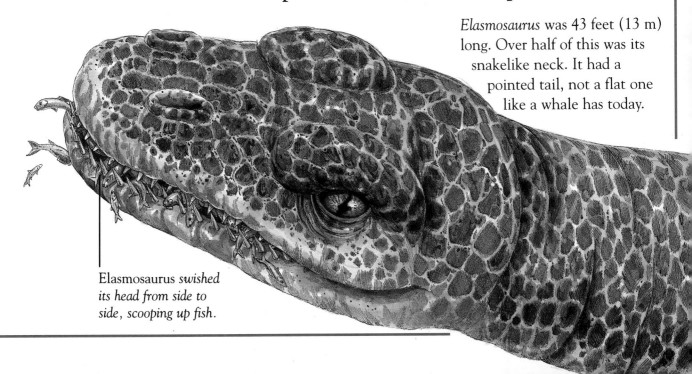

Elasmosaurus was 43 feet (13 m)
long. Over half of this was its
snakelike neck. It had a
pointed tail, not a flat one
like a whale has today.

Elasmosaurus *swished
its head from side to
side, scooping up fish.*

The meteor was about 9.5 miles (15 km) across. Most of it probably broke up in space, but as it reached earth there was a huge explosion. This created a huge cloud of dust and water vapor.

The dust cloud spread across the globe, and skies turned blood red. After that total darkness descended.

The darkness lasted for many months. The cloud may have held poisonous gases and most plants died.

Plant eaters starved slowly. The largest ones, the dinosaurs, died first – smaller ones lived longer.

About 64 million years ago,

the dinosaurs, along with most flying and swimming reptiles, disappeared forever. What disaster killed them so suddenly? Many scientists believe that a giant meteor – a chunk of rock from space – hit the earth. The skies were clogged with dust that blocked the sun and caused a darkness that may have lasted many months – maybe even years. Animals like the dinosaurs were wiped out completely.

Meat eaters ate the dead plant eaters. But these were all eaten quickly so the meat eaters starved, too.

After months, or even years, the vapor cloud lifted. Insects, small reptiles, and mammals were the only survivors.

Millions of years later, mammals and birds have developed into an incredible variety of new species.

USEFUL WORDS

Carnivore An animal that eats meat.

Cretaceous The period from 146 to 65 million years ago. Dinosaurs disappeared at the end of this period.

Cycad A palmlike plant found in tropical areas.

Fossil The preserved remains of an animal or plant that lived millions of years ago.

Hatchling A newly hatched baby animal.

Herbivore An animal that eats plants.

Ichthyosaurs Prehistoric swimming reptiles that resembled dolphins.

Jurassic The period from 208 to 146 million years ago. The biggest dinosaurs lived at this time, and the first birds developed.

Mammal A warm-blooded animal.

Mesozoic era The age of dinosaurs, from 245 to 65 million years ago.

Mongolia A large country in eastern Asia between China and Russia.

Plesiosaurs Prehistoric

swimming reptiles with long, slender bodies.

Predator An animal that hunts and preys on other animals.

Prehistoric Existing before written history began.

Prey An animal that is eaten by a predator.

Pterosaurs Prehistoric flying reptiles closely related to dinosaurs.

Triassic The period from 245 to 208 million years ago. The first dinosaurs appeared.

INDEX